Blowing Smoke

Blowing Smoke

Being a Compendium of Amusing Anecdotes,

Witty Ripostes, and Lengthy Literary Passages

on the Glories of the Cigar

COMPILED BY MARY FOLEY AND KEVIN FOLEY

PRIMA PUBLISHING

Library of Congress Cataloging-in-Publication Data

Blowing smoke: being a compendium of amusing anecdotes, witty ripostes, and lengthy literary passages on the glories of the cigar / [compiled by] Kevin and Mary Foley.

   p. cm.

   Includes index.

   ISBN 0-7615-1098-2

   1. Cigars—Quotations, maxims, etc.   2. Smoking—Quotations, maxims, etc.   I. Foley, Kevin.
     II. Foley, Mary.

PN6084.C524B58 1997

394.1'4—dc21   97-26107
                                                                    CIP

97 98 99 00 01 AA 10 9 8 7 6 5 4 3 2 1
Printed in the United States of America

How to Order

Single copies may be ordered from Prima Publishing, P.O. Box 1260BK, Rocklin, CA 95677; telephone (916) 632-4400. Quantity discounts are also available. On your letterhead, include information concerning the intended use of the books and the number of books you wish to purchase.

Visit us online at www.primapublishing.com

CONTENTS

PREFACE

The world of cigars is rich with tradition, lore, and legend. On these pages, you will find the words of some of the most prolific and colorful characters in history. If you enjoy the glories of the cigar, you have a bond with each of them. We hope that your reading will bring you closer to these great historic and literary figures, helping you discover your connection to them. Most of all, we hope that this book will boost your enjoyment of the cigars in your future.

ACKNOWLEDGMENTS

Our thanks to the great people at Prima Publishing, including Paula Munier Lee, Jennifer Basye Sander, and Karen Naungayan, for their professionalism and inspiration.

We also appreciate the many historians, librarians, tobacco growers, and tobacconists who helped us in our research from the dusty stacks of the books to the dustless highway of the Internet.

Thank you to our customers and suppliers who make The Cigar Locker "the easiest place in the world to relax" and the easiest place in the world to meet and visit with new friends.

Finally, thank you to our parents, family, and friends for their support throughout this project

CHAPTER ONE

Definitions

From The Oxford English Dictionary, *Second Edition, 1989*

C I G A R (sɪˈgaː(r)). Forms: seegar, cegar, seguar (sagar), segar, cigarre, cigar. [ad. Sp. *cigarro*: in F. *cigare.*

The Spanish word appears not to be from any lang. of W. Indies. Its close formal affinity to Sp. *cigarra* 'cicada,' naturally suggests its formation from that word, esp. as derivatives often differ merely in gender. Barcia, *Great Etymol. Spanish Dict.*, says 'el cigarro figura una cigarra de papel' (the cigar has the form of a cicada of paper). Mahn also thinks that the roll of tobacco leaf was compared to the body of the insect, which is cylindrical with a conical apex. The name *cigarral* applied to a kind of pleasure-garden and summer-house (as in the cigarrales of Toledo), which has sometimes been pressed into service in discussing the etymology, is said by Barcia, after P. Guadio, to be related neither to *cigarra* nor *cigarro,* but to be of Arabic origin meaning 'little house' (*casa pequeña*). It is said however to be applied in Cuba to a tobacco garden or nursery.]

A compact roll of tobacco-leaves for smoking, one end being taken in the mouth while the other is lit.

CIGARESQUE (sigəˈrɛsk) Having a cigar (or cigars) as a prominent feature.

CIGARILLO (sɪgəˈriləʊ). A small cigar.

"Your muleteer . . . will suspend the smoking of his cigarillo to tell some tale of Moslem gold buried."

–G. CRAYON, *Alhambra* I. 224, 1832

CIGARY (sɪˈgaːrɪ), Of or pertaining to a heavy cigar-smoker.

"A rich, port-winery, cigary voice."

–ALDOUS HUXLEY, *Antic Hay* xiv, 200, 1923

"They must appeal to rich, cigary filmtycoon me."

–DYLAN THOMAS, Letter, November 17, 1966

SMOKE-HO, SMOKE-OH, OR SMOKO. *colloq.*
(chiefly *Austral.*, *N.Z.*, and *Naut.*). A stoppage of work in order to
rest and smoke.

"Sawyers, and stockmen, carpenters, packers, shinglers and
loafers, Smoke as they work to assist them, and then knock off for
a *'smoke oh!'* "

–L. J. KENNAWAY, *Crusts*, 124, 1874

"This done, it was 'Smoke-oh!' The luxury of that rest and re-
freshment was something to be grateful for."

–F. T. BULLEN, *Cruise 'Cachalot'* viii, 1897

SMOKER ('sməʊkə(r)). A concert at which smoking is permitted.
U.S. A social gathering sometimes with organized entertainment.

"Tootling risky *apropos* songs at commercial travellers' smokers."

–JAMES JOYCE, *Finnegans Wake* 433, 1939

"Come down to our concert, A Smoker 'tis called."

–W. T. VINCENT, *Recoll. Fred Leslie* I. xviii. 25, 1894

"A smoker was scheduled frequently at which boxing bouts were featured, or a pie race, a wrestling match, [etc.]."
–E. N. ROGERS, *Queenie's Brood*, 42, 1956

"Both the tin cans and the subs have long been famed for the smokers they hold ashore."
–A. R. BOSWORTH, *My Love Affair With Navy* xii, 168, 1969

STOGY ('stəʊgɪ'). *U.S.* Now freq. stogie. Also stoga, stoggie. [Orig. *stoga,* short for *Conestoga,* the name of a town in Pennsylvania, used *attrib.* in *Conestoga wagon.*

It is alleged that *stoga boots* and *stoga cigars* were so called because they were used by the 'stoga drivers', i.e. the drivers of the Conestoga wagons plying between Wheeling and Pittsburgh.]

The distinctive epithet of a long, slender, roughly made kind of cigar or cheroot.

"The Conestoga wagon gives its name to the Stogie cigar, a great thin coarse one, supposed to have been originally a foot long and made for the delectation of the wagoner."
–J. OMWAKE, *Conestoga Six-Horse Bell Teams* 118, 1930

"It would take more'n this to keel me over,' he said, ignorant that he was lighting that terrible article, a Wheeling 'stogie'."

–RUDYARD KIPLING, *Captain Courageous*

"The man who puffs on his cigar is sucking his thumb while the man who chews vigorously on his stogie is a nail biter."

–V. PACKARD, *Hidden Persuaders*, IX, 103, 1957

CHAPTER TWO

Facts and Firsts

Cuban cigar rollers became well-versed in the classics, because the cigar factory readers often read aloud from literary works, such as stories and poetry by Victor Hugo (1802–1885).

Victor Muñoz, the journalist who established Mother's Day as a holiday, was once a reader to cigar rollers in Cuba.

Sultan Ahmed cut off the nose of any of his subjects found smoking a cigar.

Annie Oakley (1860–1926) smoked cheroots to calm her nerves before performances.

Prince Otto von Bismarck (1815–1898), the German chancellor, interrupted the Franco-Prussian War peace negotiations to praise the role of the cigar in helping to bring about an agreement. During the Battle of Königgratz, Bismarck gave the last cigar that he had with him to a dying dragoon.

Charlie Chaplin (1889–1977), as the Little Tramp in *The Gold Rush*, discovers the chewed stub of an abandoned cigar in the last scene of the film. In real life, his daughter, Geraldine Chaplin, smoked too.

Damien de Goes, Dutch explorer, is claimed to be the first to bring back tobacco seed from Florida and present it to King Sebastian of Portugal.

The explorer Cortez discovered Aztec priests in Montezuma's court, smoking *seegars* in religous rituals in 1519.

Rodrigo de Xéres, an explorer with Christopher Columbus, was the first to smoke a cigar during the first voyage, November 6, 1492, and did so every day thereafter during the exploration.

In 1793, Antoine Delpierre, French privateer, captured an entire ship-load of Dutch cigars and handed them out to citizens of Boulogne.

German spy reports of Allied naval movements during World War I were encoded to resemble orders for Havana cigars.

The match was introduced in 1805.

King Ferdinand of Bulgaria custom built a new four-cylinder Daimler limousine, the first car with an ashtray, in 1914.

The 1923 Mercedes roadster was the first car with a cigar lighter.

The one-handed, "thumb on roll bar" lighter was invented by Vernon Dunhill, brother of Alfred.

Guttersnipes, children who scoured the gutters looking for dis-banded cigar butts, often exchanged cigar bands for prizes.

In 1837, Ramón Allones, a French immigrant to Cuba, became the first tobacconist to manufacture a full-colored cigar box label and band.

Michel Ney, a marshal in Napoleon's army, is believed to be the first to request as his last wish a cigar before being executed for treason in 1815.

Edward G. Robinson was named "Mister Cigar" by American cigar importers in 1949 in recognition of the publicity he gave to the cigar in his gangster movies.

Ernest Hemingway presented Ava Gardner with a cigar band as a souvenir of their first meeting.

Amy Lowell (1874–1925), poet, critic, and author of "Patterns" and "Lilacs," was sometimes seen with a cigar in her hands or mouth. When her brother was inaugurated as president of Harvard University, she smoked cigars on stage during his address.

After a fire destroyed his Key West, Florida factory in 1869, Vincente Martínez Ybor, a successful Cuban cigar manufacturer, moved his factory to the Tampa area—and Ybor City was born.

In 1849, the *New York Times* reported that every day in New York more money was spent on cigars than bread.

The shawl-collared, silk smoking jacket evolved into the tuxedo, which to this day the French refer to as *le smoking*.

Arthur Rubinstein (1887–1982), pianist, once owned a tobacco plantation in Cuba.

Darryl F. Zanuck (1902–1979), film producer, at one time possessed interests in tobacco plantations of the Vuelta Abajo—the richest tobacco growing region in Cuba.

Pancho Villa (1878–1923) warned his gang not to smoke cigars before a raid to avoid alerting their target with the smell of smoke.

Virginia Woolf (1882–1941), British novelist and essayist, smoked with other members of the Bloomsbury Group, as did her husband, Leonard.

Urban VIII, Pope from 1623 to 1644, by papal bull forbade Spanish priests to smoke cigars.

John Wayne (1907–1979) had special cigars, larger than usual, made for his use in the Western movies in which he appeared.

José Martí, Cuban revolutionary and writer who lived in New York City from 1881 to 1895, returned to liberate Cuba from Spanish rule. He sent plans for the rebellion from Key West to Havana rolled in a cigar. Fifty years later, in 1955, Castro's supporters delivered messages hidden in cigars to Fidel in his Cuban prison cell on the Isle of Pines.

Mazzini, Italian statesman, saved his own life when he offered cigars to the men who had come to assassinate him. The villains fell to their knees to receive his pardon.

Catherine the Great (1729–1796) requested that a silk band be wrapped around her cigars so that her fingers wouldn't be soiled with tobacco stains.

Sigmund Freud (1856–1939) and Gustav Mahler (1860–1911) smoked cigars during Mahler's psychoanalysis with Freud.

It is thought that the cigar was perfected in Seville because the Spanish and Portuguese had a stronghold in South and Central America, including Cuba, while the English were exploring North America during the sixteenth and seventeenth centuries.

Peter Wendler, a German painter living in Italy, began to manufacture cigars under papal order in 1779 under a five-year concession.

John Glenn, astronaut and U.S. Senator, was awarded his weight in Cuban cigars after his history-making space flight in 1962.

CHAPTER THREE

Amusing Anecdotes,
Witty Ripostes, and
Memorable Quotes

Any cigar smoker is a friend because I know what he feels.

—ALFRED DE MUSSET (French poet and dramatist)

He who doth not smoke hath either known no great griefs, or refuseth himself the softest consolation, next to that which comes from heaven.

—E. G. BULWER-LYTTON, *What Will He Do With It?* 1859

A lone man's companion, a bachelor's friend, a hungry man's food, a sad man's cordial, a wakeful man's sleep, and a chilly man's fire . . . there's no herb like unto it under the canopy of heaven.

—CHARLES KINGSLEY, *Westward Ho!* VII, 1855

[Love] is like a cigar. If it goes out, you can light it again but it never tastes quite the same.

—LORD WAVELL (British field marshal)

When a lovely flame dies, smoke gets in your eyes.

—OTTO HARBACH, "Smoke Gets in Your Eyes" (song), 1933

I owe to the cigar a great intensification of my capacity to work and a facilitation of my self-control.

—SIGMUND FREUD

To know how to smoke is to recover certain forgotten rhythms, to re-establish communication with the self. . . .

You do not fit a cigar into your schedule; you give it a moment and it occupies your time and enriches it. . . . The pleasure of the cigar, don't forget, is not found only in the smoking. It precedes it and lingers long after the fire is out.

ZINO DAVIDOFF, *The Connoisseur's Book of the Cigar,* 1967

Do not ask me to describe the charms of reverie, or the contemplative ecstasy into which the smoke of our cigar plunges us.

–JULES SANDEAU (French novelist)

There was a young man of Herne Bay
who was making some fireworks one day:
but he dropped his cigar
in the gunpowder jar.
There was a young man of Herne Bay.

–OGDEN NASH

The blue smoke of a well-chosen cigar disappears into the air, a symbol, perhaps, of the vanity and precariousness of all things. No other object or person is capable of giving such an opportunity to indulge in introspection and to contemplate one's own being.

–ROBERT T. LEWIS

A good Cuban cigar closes the door to the vulgarities of the world.

–FRANZ LISZT (Hungarian composer)

Liszt entered a monastery near the end of his life—only after he asked and obtained the right to smoke cigars as he pleased.

I smoked tobacco and read Milton at the same time, and from the same motive—to find out what was the recondite charm in them which gave my father so much pleasure. After making myself four or five times sick with smoking, I mastered that accomplishment. . . . But I did not master Milton.

–PRESIDENT JOHN QUINCY ADAMS, 1786

A small cigar can change the world I know,
I've done it frequently at parties
Where I've won all the guests' attention
With my generosity and suave gentlemanly bearing
A little flat tin case is all you need
Breast-pocket conversation opener
And one of those ciggie lighters that look rather good
You can throw away when empty
Must be declared a great success.

–IAN ANDERSON (lead singer of Jethro Tull), *A Small Cigar*

The cigar smoker, like the perfect lover or the bagpipe player, is a calm man, slow and sure of his wind.

—MARC ALYN, critic

Now here's Bud Scott
And his old guitar,
Always smoking his big cigar.

—LOUIS ARMSTRONG, introduction of a fellow musician

The rich man has his motor car,
His country and his town estate.
He smokes a fifty-cent cigar,
And jeers at Fate.

—F. P. ADAMS, "The Rich Man"

There are two things a man never forgets—his first love and his first cigar.

Remember that silence and a good cigar are two of the finest things on earth.

–JOHN BAIN

Marilyn [Monroe] told me she liked the aroma of the cigar I was smoking—I think it was a Cohiba. So I bought her a box of small cigars.

–MILTON BERLE

At the club we had this girl: She smoked nothing but cigars. Personally, I think she only did it to make herself look older.

–MARILYN MONROE to Tom Ewell, in *The Seven Year Itch,* 1957

The British had conquered the French on Spanish soil. The cigar conquered them both.

—JEROME E. BROOKS, *The Mighty Leaf*, on the Peninsula War of 1808–1814

The man who smokes, thinks like a sage and acts like a *Samaritan*!

—E. G. BULWER-LYTTON, *Night and Morning*

And all the world's atangle and ajar,
I meditate on interstellar spaces
And smoke a mild cigar.

—HARRY DACRE (poet)

A good cigar is as great a comfort to a man as a good cry to
a woman.

−E. G. BULWER-LYTTON (English novelist, playwright, poet,
essayist, and politician), *Darnley,* 1845

It is necessary to know how to smoke so that
   one knows how to choose.
The true smoker abstains from imitating Vesuvius.
He demonstrates the requirement that during
   three-quarters of an hour
A cigar rests in his hand without going out.

−AUGUSTE BARTHÉLEMY, *L'Art de Fumer Pipe et Cigare,* 1849

But, in the matter of cigar tobacco as in life, one ought
always to be ready to revise ideas and judgment.

−ZINO DAVIDOFF, *The Connoisseur's Book of the Cigar,* 1967

If a woman knows a man's preferences, including his preference in cigars, and if a man knows what a woman likes, they will be suitably armed to face one another.

–COLETTE, *Gigi*, 1945

If alcohol is queen, then tobacco is her consort. It's a fond companion for all occasions, a loyal friend through fair weather and foul. People smoke to celebrate a happy moment, or to hide a bitter regret. Whether you're alone or with friends, it's a joy for all the senses.

–LUIS BUÑUEL (Spanish film director), *My Last Sigh*, 1984

I am sure there are many things better than a good cigar, but right now, I can't think of what they might be.

–RICHARD CARLETON HACKER, *The Ultimate Cigar Book*

[The cigar embodies] the eternal attributes of prestige, success, and *savoir faire*.

−ITALO CALVINO (novelist)

Cats may have had their goose
Cooked by tobacco-juice;
Still why deny its use
Thoughtfully taken?
We're not as tabbies are:
Smith, take a fresh cigar!
Jones, the tobacco-jar!
Here's to thee, Bacon!

−CHARLES STUART CALVERLEY (English writer), from
"Ode to Tobacco"

Viscount Montgomery: I do not drink. I do not smoke. I sleep a great deal. That is why I am in one hundred percent form.

Winston Churchill: I drink a good deal, I sleep little, and I smoke cigar after cigar. That is why I am in *two* hundred percent form.

—WINSTON CHURCHILL's retort to remark by Viscount 'General Monty' Montgomery. Churchill started smoking cigars in his early twenties and boasted of his excellent health—in spite of his habit of champagne, brandy, and cigars—throughout his ninety years.

I haven't been sick a day since I was a child. A steady diet of cigars and whiskey cured me.

—W. C. FIELDS

I must point out that my rule of life prescribed as an absolutely sacred rite smoking cigars and also the drinking of alcohol before, after, and if need be during all meals and in the intervals between them.

—WINSTON CHURCHILL, during a lunch with the Arab leader Ibn Saud, when he heard that the king's religion forbade smoking and alcohol

Yes, social friend, I love thee well,
In learned doctors' spite;
Thy clouds all other clouds dispel,
And lap me in delight.

—CHARLES SPRAGUE, "To My Cigar"

Asthma doesn't seem to bother me anymore unless I'm around cigars or dogs. The thing that would bother me most would be a dog smoking a cigar.

—STEVE ALLEN, "News Summaries," July 15, 1955

Nearly all men die of their remedies, and not of their illnesses.

—MOLIÈRE, *Le Malade Imaginaire*, 1673

Your cigars are safe, sir.

—ALFRED H. DUNHILL, 1941, telephoning Winston Churchill at 2 A.M. following the London blitz, when German bombs destroyed much of London, including Dunhill's cigar shop

Mr. Churchill's cigar has taken the place of Chamberlain's umbrella as Britain's national emblem.

He smoked about fifteen of them a day but seldom smoked one to the end. He threw them away after he had got the best out of them. I very rarely saw him without one. Hostesses invariably complained that wherever he went he left behind him a trail of cigar ash on their valuable carpets.

–PHYLLIS MOIR, *I Was Winston Churchill's Private Secretary,* 1941

There is nothing more agreeable than having a place where one can throw on the floor as many cigar butts as one pleases without the subconscious fear of a maid who is waiting like a sentinel to place an ashtray where the ashes are going to fall.

–FIDEL CASTRO

The two Christians met on the way many people who were going to their towns, women and men, with a firebrand in the hand, [and] herbs to drink the smoke thereof, as they are accustomed.

—CHRISTOPHER COLUMBUS, navigation diary entry, November 6, 1492, *Journal of the First Voyage (El Libro de la Primer Navegación),*—an abstract from Columbus' original onboard journal written by Bartolomé de Las Casas in the early 1500s.

Some historians consider the Columbus diary entry to be the first historical account of cigar-like smoking of tobacco.

[They use] a lighted piece of coal and some grasses, and inhale the aroma using catapults which in their language they call *tabacos.*

—LUIS DE TORRES, an interpreter and crew member under Christopher Columbus, 1492

The Indians used a Y-shaped tube, putting the two ends of the fork up their nostrils, and the tube in the burning grasses.

—GONZALO FERNÁNDEZ DE OVIEDO Y VALDÉS, *History and Natural History of the West Indies*, 1535

People were "drinking smoke." There were "chimney men" who carried a brown tube burning at one end. They drank from the other end and smoke came out.

—RODRIGO DE XÉRES, a crew member under Christopher Columbus, 1492

What a blessing this smoking is! Perhaps the greatest that we owe to the discovery of America.

—SIR ARTHUR HELPS (English essayist and historian), *Friends in Council*

I have met many alchemists who have let gold go up in
smoke, but only you, Sir Walter, have I seen transmute
smoke into gold.

—ELIZABETH I to Sir Walter Raleigh upon his success in growing
tobacco in the Virginia colony (unfortunately, James I later sent Raleigh
to the gallows)

Gentlemen, you may smoke.

—EDWARD VII OF ENGLAND, upon his succession to the
throne in 1901 (his mother, Queen Victoria, had banned the smoking of
cigars in her presence and therefore in her court or society, reinforcing
the policy of James I)

Lady Bracknell: Do you smoke?
Earnest: Well, yes, I must admit I smoke.

Lady Bracknell: I am glad to hear it. A man should always have an occupation of some kind.

–OSCAR WILDE, *The Importance of Being Earnest*, 1899

Oscar Wilde was a member of King Edward's crowd—he was allowed to smoke!

These Gentlemen [three friars at Nicaragua] gave us some Seegars to smoke . . . These are Leaves of Tobacco rolled up in such Manner that they serve both for a Pipe and Tobacco itself. These the ladies, as well as gentlemen, are very fond of smoking . . . they know no other way [of smoking] here, for there is no such Thing as a Tobacco-Pipe throughout New Spain.

–J. COCKBURN, *Journal over Land*, 1735

The Spanish in Europe preferred the cigar. Pipe smoking
was not popular in Spain in the seventeenth century as it was
in England, Holland, and Germany.

—SARAH AUGUSTA DICKSON

Some of them [Seville cigar girls] resolutely carried a cigar
at an angle in their mouths with all the aplomb of a cavalry
officer; others, O God, chewed tobacco like old sailors because they were allowed to have all the tobacco they wanted
which could be consumed where they worked.

—THÉOPHILE GAUTIER, *Voyage en Espagne*

[Of the female cigar rollers in the Seville cigar factories]
most wear a blouse (they are the prudes); almost all work
with their breasts exposed, wearing a simple cloth skirt

which is sometimes tucked up around the thighs. There are some, to be sure, unattractive bodies among this group, but all were interesting and I stopped often before a most beautiful woman—with a full bosom, clear shining skin ...

—PIERRE LOUŸS (poet and novelist), *La Femme et le Pantin,* 1898

Don Juan took out a Seville cigar and called for a light when meeting the devil, who was traveling along the opposite bank of the river Guadalquivir.

—From DON JUAN as told by PROSPER MÉRIMÉE

The ash of a cigar has always been sacred. It is wrong to demand a light from those who lovingly contemplate the long ash of a Havana ...The conversation of cigar smoking ought to be slow and majestic.

—EUGENE MARSAN

Presently I was qualified. I had already published a novel and it had had an unexpected success. I thought my fortune was made, and, abandoning medicine to become a writer, I went to Spain. I was then twenty-three. I was much more ignorant than are, it seems to me, young men of that age at the present day. I settled down in Seville. I grew a moustache, smoked Filipino cigars, learnt the guitar, bought a broad-brimmed hat with a flat crown, in which I swaggered down the Sierpes, and hankered for a flowing cape, lined with green and red velvet. But on account of the expense I did not buy it . . . I fell in love with Seville and the life one led there.

—SOMERSET MAUGHAM, from *The Summing Up,* 1938

It's difficult to be bad-tempered with a good cigar in one's mouth.

Like many luxuries, cigars have acquired vulgar connotations of status. You know perfectly well that you should never agree to be photographed cigar in hand for the business pages unless you want to be branded a capitalist pig. It's quite unjust really—you wonder what the *Wall Street Journal* would make of Fidel Castro. But cigars in art have also signified an attainable pleasure that transcends class . . . It seems cigars in art represent not merely a rich life, but a life richly lived, irrespective of one's tax bracket.

—SIR TERENCE CONRAN (British designer and businessman)

Pull out a Montecristo at a dinner party, and the political liberal turns into the nicotine fascist.

—MARTYN HARRIS, British journalist and author, *The Daily Telegraph* (London), January 20, 1989

Well, boys, I'll tell you what I think. The convention will be deadlocked. After the other candidates have failed, we'll get together in some smoke-filled hotel room, oh, about 2:11 in the morning, and some fifteen men, bleary-eyed with lack of sleep, will sit down around a big table and when that time comes Senator Harding will be selected.

—HARRY M. DAUGHERTY (Republican Party political strategist and attorney general under President Warren Harding), to reporters on the eve of the Republican National Convention, July 1920

The "smoke-filled" hotel room referred to was George Harvey's suite, rooms 804 and 805, at the Blackstone Hotel, Chicago. Later, Daugherty maintained that he had not said "smoke-filled."

In the future all men will be able to smoke Havanas.

—HERR DOKTOR SCHUTTE (physician and early Marxist)

You better take advantage of the good cigars. You don't get much else in that job.

–THOMAS P. (TIP) O'NEILL (Speaker of the House), to Vice President Walter F. Mondale, quoted in *Time*, June 4, 1984

Sometimes a cigar is just a cigar.

–SIGMUND FREUD

My boy! Smoking is one of the greatest and cheapest enjoyments in life, and if you decide in advance not to smoke, I can only feel sorry for you.

–SIGMUND FREUD to his seventeen-year-old nephew Harry after he declined a cigar

This little ol' cigar is my only vice. Cause I needed a vice in the joint to remind me I was human.

—ROBERT DENIRO (as Max Cady) to Nick Nolte
(as Sam Bowden) in *Cape Fear,* 1991

By the cigars they smoke, and the composers they love, ye shall know the texture of men's souls.

—JOHN GALSWORTHY, *Indian Summer of a Forsyte*

A man's shoes will tell you if he has money; his clothes if he has style. But if you want to know if he's a sport, see if he is wearing a good cigar.

—NAT SHERMAN

Floating away like the fountains' spray,
Or the snow-white plume of a maiden,
The smoke-wreaths rise to the starlit skies
With blissful fragrance laden.
Then smoke away till a golden ray
Lights up the dawn of the morrow,
For a cheerful cigar, like a shield will bar
The blows of care and sorrow.

—FRANCIS MILES FINCH

That night I was in the living room smoking a cigar and
drinking a whiskey and water and listening to Gracie Allen
on the radio. The girls had gone to the show and sitting
there I felt sleepy and I felt good.

—ERNEST HEMINGWAY, *To Have and Have Not*, 1937

Light a cigar and let me expound.

I gathered up some scattered ash from the floor. It was dark in colour and flaky—such an ash is only made by a Trichinopoly. I have made a special study of cigar ashes—in fact, I have written a monograph upon the subject. I flatter myself that I can distinguish at a glance the ash of any known brand either of cigar or of tobacco. It is just in such details that the skilled detective differs from the Gregson and Lestrade type.

—SHERLOCK HOLMES in Sir Arthur Conan Doyle, *A Study in Scarlet,* 1887

Tobacco is the opiate of the gentleman, the religion of the rich.

—GUILLERMO CABRERA INFANTE, *Holy Smoke,* 1985

Cigarettes are for chain-smoking, cigars must be smoked one at time, peaceably, with all the leisure in the world. Cigarettes are of the instant, cigars are for eternity.

—GUILLERMO CABRERA INFANTE (Cuban novelist), 1985

Tobacco is a dirty weed: I like it.
It satisfies no normal need: I like it.
It makes you think, it makes you lean,
It takes the hair right off your bean;
It's the worst darn stuff I've ever seen:
I like it.

—GRAHAM HEMMINGER, "Tobacco," in Penn State *Froth,*
November 1915

For thy sake, Tobacco, I
Would do anything but die.

—CHARLES LAMB, from "A Farewell to Tobacco"

If you smoke too much, you will become drunk as with a
strong wine . . . I found this out for myself.

—BARTOLOMÉ DE LAS CASAS, Dominican friar and chronicler, of Columbus and his crew, 1550

People smoke for their mental health, don't they? It's part of
their total health, I'd say.

—DAVID HOCKNEY (British artist), interview in *The Guardian*,
March 25, 1995

On September 13, 1862, Union soldiers Private Barton W. Mitchell and Sergeant John M. Bloss found a piece of paper wrapped around three cigars at their campsite outside of Frederick, Maryland. The piece of paper turned out to be a copy of Confederate General Robert E. Lee's orders for the invasion of Maryland, lost by the Southerners as they left the city. Passed up through the chain of command, the captured order gave Union General George B. McClellan advanced notice of his enemy's movements. Holding the paper, McClellan exclaimed, "Here is a paper with which, if I cannot whip Bobby Lee, I will be willing to go home."

—As described at the Antietam National Battlefield, National Park Service

Prowling in Regent Street towards evening, whiskered and cigared.

—E.G. BULWER-LYTTON, 1830

As many as ten thousand [cigars] were soon received. I gave
away all that I could get rid of, but having such a quantity
on hand I naturally smoked more than I would have done
under ordinary circumstances, and I have continued the
habit ever since.

–ULYSSES S. GRANT, on the kind gesture of Union supporters
who sent cigars showing support for the troops

When Fear and Care and grim Despair
Flock round me in a ghostly crowd,
One charm dispels them all in air,–
I blow my after-dinner cloud.

–HENRY S. LEIGH

But after all I try in vain

To fetter my opinion;

Since each upon my giddy brain

Has boasted a dominion.

Comparisons, I'll not provoke

Lest *all* should be offended.

Let this discussion end in smoke

As many more have ended.

–HENRY S. LEIGH

What this country needs is a really good five-cent cigar.

–THOMAS RILEY MARSHALL, Vice President of the United States under Woodrow Wilson, 1919

Marshall made this whispered side remark (to Rose, the Assistant Secretary of the Senate) while presiding over a Senate debate on the needs of the country.

Our country has plenty of good five-cent cigars, but the trouble is they charge fifteen cents for them.

—WILL ROGERS (humorist)

What voluptuousness . . . when I lunched with my father, in the last century, at Bignon or Paillard. After finishing the meal, he produced boxes of sparkling cigars: Valle, Clay, Upmann. I opened these boxes which evoked visions of dancing girls, and I removed the bands, because that is what is to be done.

—STÉPHANE MALLARMÉ (French poet)

If the birth of a genius resembles that of an idiot, the end of a Havana Corona resembles that of a five-cent cigar.

—SACHA GUITRY (French actor and dramatist)

The warmth of thy glow
Well-lighted cigar
Makes happy thoughts flow,
And drives sorrow afar.

Sweet cheer of sadness!
Life's own happy star!
I greet thee with gladness,
My friendly cigar!

—FRIEDRICH MARC, "To My Cigar"

What smells so? Has somebody been burning a Rag, or is there a Dead Mule in the Back yard? No, the Man is Smoking a Five-Cent Cigar.

—EUGENE FIELD, (American writer and journalist)
"The Five-Cent Cigar," in *The Tribune Primer*

Play ball!

–THOMAS RILEY MARSHALL, U.S. Vice President, holding a cigar in one hand and throwing out the first ball with the other during Baseball Opening Day ceremonies, Washington D.C., April 15, 1918.

The Cuban climate gave to tobacco grown there the best aroma in the world and to the Cubans the most beautiful skin.

–HERMAN MELVILLE (British novelist and playwright)

The *a priori* opinion of that juror who smokes the worst cigars.

–H. L. MENCKEN, *A Book of Burlesques*

Let Aristotle and all your philosophers say what they like,
there is nothing to be compared with tobacco. . .
There is nothing like tobacco;
it is the passion of all decent people;
someone who lives without tobacco
does not deserve to live.

– MOLIÉRE (French playwright), *Don Juan*, 1665

He sat at the Algonquin, smoking a cigar.
A coffin of a clock bonged out the time.
She was ten minutes late. But in that time,
He puffed the blue eternity of his cigar.

– HOWARD MOSS, from *At the Algonquin*

Above the smoke and stir of this dim spot which men call
earth.

–JOHN MILTON (English poet), *Comus,* 1634

Cognac and cigars ... it's like finding the perfect woman.
When you've got her, why go chasing after another?

–MICHAEL NOURI (actor)

The light ones may be killers,

And the dark ones may be mild;

Not the wrappers but the fillers,

Make cigars or women wild.

–KEITH PRESTON, "Popular Fallacies"

When smoking began to go out of fashion, learning began to go out of fashion also.

—RICHARD PORSON (English scholar)

Here, here have a cigar. Go on, light it up and be somebody.

—An unidentified extra to Jack Webb (as jazz band leader Pete Kelly) in the film *Pete Kelly's Blues,* 1955

He always liked to chew some, when writing something gruesome.

—EDMUND BENTLEY, On Poe

Prince Rainier of Monaco: Onassis judges Havanas by their length.

Aristotle Onassis: And the Prince chooses them by their band.

–ZINO DAVIDOFF, *Connoisseur's Book of the Cigar*, 1967
Reportedly a conversation between Onassis—who outfitted his yacht,
Christina *with a humidor—and Prince Ranier.*

Crimson is the slow smolder of the cigar end I hold,
Gray is the ash that stiffens and covers all silent the fire.
(A great man I know is dead and while he lies in his
   coffin a gone flame
I sit here in cumbering shadows and smoke and watch my
   thoughts come and go.)

–CARL SANDBURG, "Crimson," from *Chicago Poems,* 1916

You smile and you smoke your cigar, my boy;
You walk with a languid swing;
You tinkle and tune your guitar, my boy,
And lift up your voice and sing;
The midnight moon is a friend of yours,
And a serenade your joy—
And it's only an age like mine that cures
A trouble like yours, my boy!

–JAMES WHITCOMB RILEY, "My Boy"

The cigar is the perfect complement to an elegant lifestyle.

The cigar numbs sorrow and fills the solitary hours with a million gracious images.

–GEORGE SAND (French novelist)

"Now look," she said, "either dance with me—or the cigar."

Sammy jerked the cigar from his mouth as if it were a stopper checking his flow of words.

–BUDD WILSON SCHULBERG,
What Makes Sammy Run?, 1941

Cigars after dinner are delightful, Smoking before breakfast
is unnatural.

–GEORGE BERNARD SHAW

On a cold morning in winter a Toscan cigar fortifies the soul.

–STENDHAL (French writer), from his journal, circa 1838

My ashes, as the phoenix, may bring forth
A bird that will revenge upon you all.

—WILLIAM SHAKESPEARE, *Henry VI*, 1592

They had no good cigars there, my lord; and I left the place
in disgust.

—ALFRED, LORD TENNYSON (English poet), while visiting
Venice

I vow and believe that the cigar has been one of the greatest
creature comforts of my life—a kind companion, a gentle
stimulant, an amiable anodyne, a cementer of friendship.

—WILLIAM MAKEPEACE THACKERAY (English novelist)

My days have crackled and gone up in smoke.

–FRANCIS THOMPSON, "The Hound of Heaven," 1893

The cigar, like the pipe, ought to match your physique.

–KEES VAN DONGEN (French painter)

Tobacco is a filthy weed,

That from the devil does proceed;

It drains your purse, it burns your clothes,

And makes a chimney of your nose.

–Attributed to BENJAMIN WATERHOUSE (physician), by Oliver

Wendell Holmes (physician and author)

The most futile and disastrous day seems well spent when it is reviewed through the blue, fragrant smoke of a Havana cigar.

Worked quite well. Drank good wine and smoked good cigars.

—EVELYN WAUGH (English author)

All bitter things conduce to sweet,
As this example shows;
Without the little spirochete
We'd have no chocolate to eat,
Nor would tobacco's fragrance greet
The European nose.

—RICHARD PURDY WILBUR, *Pangloss's Song: A Comic Opera Lyric,* 1961

Stalin, Truman and Churchill came before St. Peter for adjudication. When they had passed the test the good saint offered to give each of them anything he wanted.

"I want the Americans to go home," said Stalin.

"And I want Russia destroyed," snapped Truman.

There was a twinkle in Churchill's eye and a sly smile on his cherubic face. "Is this on the level?" he asked. "Anything I want?"

"Yes, anything," answered St. Peter. "Well, then," said Churchill, "I'll just have a cigar. But serve these other gentlemen first."

–LELAND D. BALDWIN, *The Meaning of America*

Paul: What was it that gave you the idea to do this project?

Augie: I don't know, just came to me. It's my corner, after all. I mean it's just one little part of the world, but things take place there too, just like anywhere else. It's a record of my little spot.
—WILLIAM HURT and HARVEY KEITEL, in *Smoke* when Augie Wren explains to Paul Benjamin why he has taken a picture from his cigar store every day at the same time for many years

Customer: Gee, this cigar is rotten!
Storekeeper: Well, you shouldn't complain. You've got only one of them. I've got a thousand of the darned things.
—From *Stories for Speaking*

Cigars are my inspiration, the bigger the better then.

—ORSON WELLES (actor, producer, and director)

ANONYMOUS QUOTES

Smoking a cigar will "clear the air."

An optimist is a man who thinks his wife has stopped smoking cigarettes when he finds cigar butts around the house.

A passenger on a commuter train asked the conductor, "Is smoking permitted, Mister?"

"No," the skipper told him.

"Well, where did all these butts and all this smoke come from?"

The man in uniform replied, "From people who didn't ask questions."

Cigar smoking knows no politics. It's about the pursuit of pleasure, taste, and aroma.

It's better for a person to be smoking here on earth than in the hereafter.

As ye smoke, so shall ye reek.

Some men smoke between meals, others eat between smokes.

Many a man's idea of giving up smoking is merely giving up buying.

Smoke and the world smokes with you, swear off and you smoke alone.

Inscription on gift cigarette lighter: "To my matchless girl friend."

No cigar is so bad that sooner or later it won't meet its match.

The man who turns over a new leaf has probably changed his brand of cigars.

CHAPTER FOUR

Lengthy Literary Passages

George Burns (1896–1996)

George Burns is the only celebrity with both his hands and his cigar imprinted in front of Mann's (formally Grauman's) Chinese Theatre on Hollywood Boulevard.

At a Las Vegas hotel in which George Burns frequently appeared, the following sign was posted: "No smoking for all persons under the age of ninety-five." The message on the sign was inspired by the exception passed for the card room of The Hillcrest Country Club in West Los Angeles, where Burns was a member.

From George Burns: The First 100 Years, *1996*

George (Burns) and Jack (Benny) used to frequent Chasen's restaurant in Beverly Hills. One night while they were dining there with their wives Gracie and Mary, Jack said, "Let's get Dave Chasen to pick up the check tonight." "How do we do that, Jack?" George asked. "We're probably his best customers," Jack answered, "so after dinner I'll call him over and tell him, 'Dave, if George Burns pays this check, I'm never coming in here again.' Then you say, 'And if Jack pays this check, I won't come in here again.' You know Dave, he'll say, 'Fellas, stop fighting,' and he'll pick it up." George said, "Jack, it's a great idea. It can't miss."

Finally when dinner was over Jack called Dave Chasen over to the table and told him, "If George Burns gets this check, I'm not coming in here again." Jack then looked over at George who smiled at Jack, took a long puff on his cigar, smiled at Dave Chasen, and said nothing. Needless to say, Jack fell to the floor laughing.

Mark Twain (1835–1910)

Cigar smokers, as a general rule, are very polite people.

If I cannot smoke in heaven, then I shall not go.

I smoke in moderation—only one cigar at a time.

Eating and sleeping are the only activities that should be allowed to interrupt a man's enjoyment of his cigar.

To cease smoking is the easiest thing I ever did. I ought to know because I've done it a thousand times.

I pledged myself to smoke but one cigar a day. I kept the cigar waiting until bedtime, then I had a luxurious time with it. But desire persecuted me every day and all day long. I found myself hunting for larger cigars . . . within the month my cigar had grown to such proportions that I could have used it as a crutch.

From Mark Twain's "Seventieth Birthday Dinner Speech,"
Delmonico's restaurant, New York, 1905

I have made it a rule never to smoke more than one cigar at a time. I have no other restrictions as regards smoking. I do not know just when I began to smoke, I only know that it was in my father's lifetime, and that I was discreet. He passed from this life early in 1847, when I was a shade past eleven; ever since then I have smoked publicly. As an example to others, and not that I care for moderation myself, it has always been my rule never to smoke when asleep, and never to refrain when awake. It is a good rule. I mean, for me; but some of you know quite well that it wouldn't answer for everybody that's trying to get to be seventy.

. . . Today it is all of sixty years since I began to smoke the limit. I have never bought cigars with life belts around them. I early found that those were too expensive for me. I have always bought cheap cigars—reasonably cheap, at any rate. Sixty years ago they cost me four dollars a barrel, but my taste has improved, latterly, and I pay seven now. Six or seven. Seven, I think, Yes, it's seven. But that includes the barrel. I often have smoking parties at my house; but the people that come have always just taken the pledge. I wonder why that is?

As for drinking, I have no rule about that. When the others drink I like to help; otherwise I remain dry, by habit and preference. This dryness does not hurt me, but it could easily hurt you, because you are different. You let it alone.

. . . I desire now to repeat and emphasize that maxim: We can't reach old age by another man's road. My habits protect my life but they would assassinate you.

Groucho Marx (1890-1977)

Groucho Marx made the *unlit* cigar a famous stage prop.

When asked why he used cigars in his routines, Groucho Marx responded, "It gave you time to think. You could tell a joke and if the audience didn't laugh you could take some puffs on the cigar."

And if the joke wasn't funny?

"Then we used a different cigar."

If I have to choose between a woman and a cigar, I will always choose the cigar.

When asked by his wife to give up his cigars, Groucho replied, "No, but we can remain friends."

Contestant on *You Bet Your Life* with nineteen children: I love my wife.

Groucho Marx, taking his cigar out of his mouth: I love my cigar, but I take it out once in a while.

Rudyard Kipling (1865–1936)

"The Betrothed," in Departmental Ditties, *1899*

Open the old cigar-box, get me a Cuba stout,
For things are running crossways, and Maggie and I are out.
We quarrelled about Havanas—we fought o'er a
    good cheroot,
And I know she is exacting, and she says I am a brute.
Open the old cigar-box—let me consider a space;
In the soft blue veil of the vapour musing Maggie's face.
Maggie is pretty to look at—Maggie's a loving lass,
But the prettiest cheeks must wrinkle, the truest of loves
    must pass.
There's peace in a Laranaga, there's calm in a Henry Clay,
But the best cigar in an hour is finished and thrown away—
Thrown away for another as perfect and ripe and brown—

But I could not throw away Maggie for fear o' the talk o'
   the town!

Maggie, my wife at fifty—grey and dour and old—

With never another Maggie to purchase for love or gold!

And the light of Days that have Been the dark of the Days
   that Are,

And Love's torch stinking and stale, like the butt of a dead
   cigar—

The butt of a dead cigar you are bound to keep in your
pocket—

With never a new one to light tho' it's charred and black to
   the socket!

Open the old cigar-box—let me consider awhile

Here is a mild Manilla—there is a wifely smile.

Which is the better portion—bondage bought with a ring,

Or a harem of dusky beauties fifty tied in a string?

Counsellors cunning and silent—comforters true and tried,

And never a one of the fifty to sneer at a rival bride.

Thought in the early morning, solace in time of woes,

Peace in the hush of the twilight, balm ere my eyelids close.

This will the fifty give me, asking naught in return,

With only a Suttee's passion—to do their duty and burn.

This will the fifty give me. When they are spent and dead,

Five times other fifties shall be my servants instead.

The furrows of far-off Java, the isles of the Spanish Main,

When they hear my harem is empty will send me my

    brides again.

I will take no heed to their raiment, nor food for their

    mouths withal,

So long as the gulls are nesting, so long as the showers fall.

I will scent 'em with best Vanilla, with tea will I temper

    their hides,

And the Moor and the Mormon shall envy who read of the
    tale of my brides.
For Maggie has written a letter to give me my choice between
The wee little whimpering Love and the great god
    Nick o' Teen.
And I have been servant of Love for barely a
    twelvemonth clear,
But I have been Priest of Partagas a matter of seven year;
And the gloom of my bachelor days is flecked with the
    cheery light
Of stumps that I burned to Friendship and Pleasure and
Work and Fight.
And I turn my eyes to the future that Maggie and I
    must prove,

But the only light on the marshes is the Will-o'-the-Wisp
  of Love.
Will it see me safe through my journey or leave me bogged
  in the mire?
Since a puff of tobacco can cloud it, shall I follow the
  fitful fire?
Open the old cigar-box—let me consider anew—
Old friends, and who is Maggie that I should abandon *you?*
A million surplus Maggies are willing to bear the yoke;
And a woman is only a woman, but a good cigar is a Smoke.
Light me another Cuba—I hold to my first-sworn vows,
If Maggie will have no rival, I'll have no Maggie for Spouse!

Samuel Low

"To a Segar"

Sweet antidote to sorrow, toil and strife,

Charm against discontent and wrinkled care,

Who knows thy power can never know despair;

Who knows thee not, one solace lacks of life:

When cares oppress, or when the busy day

Gives place to tranquil eve, a single puff

Can drive ev'n want and lassitude away,

And give a mourner happiness enough.

From thee when curling clouds of incense rise,

They hide each evil that in prospect lies;

But when in evanescence fades thy smoke,

Ah! what, dear sedative, my cares shall smother?

If thou evaporate, the charm is broke,

Till I, departing taper, light another.

H. G. WELLS (1866–1946)

From The Invisible Man, *1897*

After he had done eating, and he made a heavy meal, the Invisible Man demanded a cigar. He bit the end savagely before Kemp could find a knife, and cursed when the outer leaf loosened. It was strange to see him smoking; his mouth, and throat, pharynx and nares, became visible as a sort of whirling smoke cast.

"This blessed gift of smoking!" he said, and puffed vigorously. "I'm lucky to have fallen upon you, Kemp. You must help me. Fancy tumbling on you just now! I'm in a devilish scrape. I've been mad, I think. The things I have been through! But we will do things yet. Let me tell you—"

He helped himself to more whiskey and soda. Kemp got up, looked about him, and fetched himself a glass from his spare room. "It's wild—but I suppose I may drink."

"You haven't changed much, Kemp these dozen years. You fair men don't. Cool and methodical after the first collapse, I must tell you. We will work together!"

"But how was it all done?" said Kemp, "and how did you get like this?"

"For God's sake, let me smoke in peace for a little while! And then I will begin to tell you."

PROSPER MÈRIMÈE (1803–1870)

From the opera Carmen, *Act I*

The story takes place in Seville with its cigar factories. Carmen is a Gypsy cigar roller.

Believing that I ought not to take offense at the lack of concern he seemed to show at my coming, I stretched out on the

grass and, in a very casual manner, asked this stranger with
the gun whether he had a tinderbox on him. At the same
time I pulled out my cigar case. The stranger, still without
speaking, fumbled in his pocket, took out his tinderbox,
and hastened to give me a light. Evidently he was becoming
a little more human, for he sat down before me—not, however, without his musket. When my cigar was lit, I picked out
the best one among those I had left and asked him if he
smoked.

"Yes sir," he replied.

These were the first words that he spoke, and I noticed that
he did not pronounce the "s" in the Andalusian manner. I
concluded, therefore, that he was a traveller like myself, only
less of an archaeologist.

"You'll find this one quite good," I told him, handing him a genuine Havana Royal.

With a slight bow of his head, he lit his cigar from mine, thanked me with another nod, and then began to smoke, apparently with very great pleasure.

"Ah!" he exclaimed, letting the smoke of his first puff slowly escape through his mouth and nostrils, "how long it's been since I've had a smoke!"

In Spain, a cigar given and accepted establishes relations of hospitality, as does the sharing of bread and salt in the Orient.

From Carmen, *Act II*

One evening at the hour when one can see nothing more, I
was quietly smoking and leaning against the parapet of the
embankment when a woman came up the stairway which
leads to the river and sat down near me. In her hair she had
a spray of jasmine, the petals of which diffuse an intoxicating
perfume in the evening air. She was simply, indeed even
poorly dressed, entirely in black, as are most of the working
girls in the evening. Proper women wear black only in the
morning; in the evening they dress á la francesa.

When she reached me, my bathing girl let the mantilla
which covered her head slip down on her shoulders. In
the dim starlight I saw that she was petite, young, and that
she had a shapely figure and very big eyes. I threw away my
cigar at once. She understood this highly French gesture of

politeness, and hastened to tell me that she liked the smell of tobacco very much and that she herself even smoked when she found some very mild papelitos. Fortunately, I had some like that in my cigarette case, and I hastened to offer one to her. She deigned to take it and lit it from an end of a burning piece of rope which a child brought to us at the cost of a penny.

Blending the smoke of our two cigarettes, the bathing beauty and I chatted so long that the two of us found ourselves almost alone on the embankment. I thought that I was not being too forward when I offered to take her for some ice-cream at a nearby nevería [cafe].

WALLACE STEVENS (1879–1955)

From "The Emperor of Ice-Cream," 1923

Call the roller of big cigars,
The muscular one, and bid him whip
In kitchen cups concupiscent curds.
Let the wenches dawdle in such dress
As they are used to wear, and let the boys
Bring flowers in last month's newspapers.
Let be be finale of seem.
The only emperor is the emperor of ice-cream.

Duc de la Rochefoucauld-Liancourt

From his sea voyage journal, 1794

The Duke was sent to America on a special mission to present a message from the French revolutionary government.

The cigar is a great resource. It is necessary to have traveled for a long time on a ship to understand that at least the cigar affords you the pleasure of smoking. It raises your spirits. Are you troubled by something? The cigar dissolves it. Are you subject to aches and pains (or bad temper)? The cigar will change your disposition. Are you harassed by unpleasant thoughts? Smoking a cigar puts one in a frame of mind to dispense with these. Do you ever feel a little faint from hunger? A cigar satisfies the yearning. If you are obsessed by sad thoughts, a cigar will take your mind off of them. Finally don't you sometimes have some pleasant remembrance or consoling thought? A cigar will reinforce this. Sometimes they die out, and happy are those who do not need to relight too quickly. I hardly need to say anything more about the cigar, to which I dedicate this little eulogy for past services rendered.

ROBERT LOUIS STEVENSON (1850–1894)

From Virginibus Puerisque, *1881*

Lastly (and this is, perhaps, the golden rule), no woman should marry a teetotaler, or a man who does not smoke.

It is not for nothing that this "ignoble tabagie," as Michelet calls it, spreads over all the world. Michelet rails against it because it renders you happy apart from thought or work; to provident women this will seem no evil influence in married life. Whatever keeps a man in the front garden, whatever checks wondering fancy and all inordinate ambition, whatever makes for lounging and contentment, makes just so surely for domestic happiness.

From The Sinking Ship

"Sir," said the first lieutenant, bursting into the Captain's cabin, "the ship is going down."

"Very well, Mr. Spoker," said the Captain, "but that is no reason for going about half-shaved. Exercise your mind a moment, Mr. Spoker, and you will see that to the philosophic eye there is nothing new in our position: the ship (if she is to go down at all) may be to have been going down since she was first launched."

"She is settling fast," said the first lieutenant, as he returned from shaving.

... "I beg pardon, sir," said Mr. Spoker, "but what is precisely the difference between shaving in a sinking ship and smoking in a powder magazine?"

"Or doing anything at all in any conceivable circumstance? cried the Captain. "Perfectly conclusive; give me a cigar!"

Two minutes afterwards the ship blew up with glorious detonation.

BRET HARTE (1836–1902)

From John Jenkins; *or,* The Smoker Reformed

"One cigar a day!" said Judge Boompointer. "One cigar a day!" repeated John Jenkins, as with trepidation he dropped his half-consumed cigar under his work-bench.

"One cigar a day is three cents a day," remarked Judge Boom-pointer, gravely, "and do you know, sir, what one cigar a day, or three cents a day, amounts to in the course of four years?"

John Jenkins, in his boyhood, had attended the village school, and possessed considerable arithmetical ability. Taking up a shingle which lay upon his workbench, and producing a piece of chalk, with a feeling of conscious pride he made an exhaustive calculation:

"Exactly forty-three dollars and eighty cents," he replied, wiping the perspiration from his heated brow, while his face flushed with honest enthusiasm.

"Well, sir, if you saved three cents a day, instead of wasting it, you would now be the possessor of a new suit of clothes, an illustrated Family Bible, a pew in the church, a complete set of Patent Office reports, a hymn-book, and a paid subscription to *Arthur's Home Magazine*, which could be purchased for exactly forty-three dollars and eighty cents—and," added the Judge, with increasing sternness, "if you calculate leap year, which you seem to have strangely omitted—you have three cents more, sir; three cents more! What would that buy you, sir?"

"A cigar," suggested John Jenkins.

Joseph Warren Fabens

"My Last Cigar"

Twas off the blue Canary Isles
A glorious summer day,
I sat upon the quarter deck,
And whiffed my cares away;
And as the volumed smoke arose,
Like incense in the air,
I breathed a sigh to think, in sooth,
It was my last cigar.
I watched the ashes as it came
Fast drawing to the end;
I watched it as a friend would watch
Beside a dying friend;
But still the flame swept slowly on;
It vanished into air;

I threw it from me,—spare the tale,—
It was my last cigar.
I've seen the land of all I love
Fade in the distance dim;
I've watched above the blighted heart,
Where once proud hope hath been;
But I've never known a sorrow
That could with that compare,
When off the blue Canaries
I smoked my last cigar.

About the Authors

Kevin and Mary Foley are the owners of The Cigar Locker of Granite Bay, a cigar store and wine bar hidden in the Sierra Foothills of Northern California's wine country—just off Interstate 80, halfway between San Francisco and Lake Tahoe.

Kevin began in the cigar business handcrafting humidors under the name Napa Cigar Humidor. In February of 1995 he became one of the very first to offer cigar humidors on the World Wide Web. After some time of commerce on the Internet, Kevin found that he also wanted to do something more connected to the local community. In August of 1996, Kevin and Mary opened The Cigar Locker in a historic farmhouse in a beautiful and natural setting. The rest, you might say, is history.

Kevin and Mary hope you'll visit them sometime soon at The Cigar Locker of Granite Bay or at their Web site www.cigarlocker.com.

Mary, a California native, has a B.S. and an M.B.A. from Stanford University. Kevin, a Connecticut native, has a B.A. from Bard College.